THE CONFIDENT HOME COOK

Dress to Impress

(Your Salad, That Is!)

Your Flavorful, Fun *(and Slightly Sassy)*
Guide to Homemade Vinaigrettes and Salad Dressings That Wow

Kerstin Decook

THE CONFIDENT HOME COOK
Dress to Impress (Your Salad, That Is!)
© 2025 Kerstin Decook. All Rights Reserved

For information about this title or to order other books and/or electronic media, contact the publisher.

Publisher Info:
Rock The Kitchen
Become A Confident Home Cook
Email: decook@rockthekitchen.net
Website: www.rockthekitchen.net

Paperback ISBN: 979-8-9989774-0-4
eBook ISBN: 979-8-9989774-1-1

Library of Congress Control Number: 2025910501

Printed in the United States of America.

Cover illustration artist: Yvette Gilbert from the United Kingdom
Interior illustration artist: Amitha Arun from the United Arab Emirates
Book cover design and interior formatting: Van-garde Imagery, Inc.

Contents

From Me to You

Hey there, friend —

Before we jump into the world of whisking, drizzling, dipping, and full-on dressing domination, I just want to say *thank you* for picking up this book.

Whether you're here because you're salad-curious, flavor-hungry, aiming for healthier eating, more nutritious meals, less waste (goodbye plastic bottles!), or simply want a more cost-effective and creative way to enjoy food — you're in exactly the right place.

This book was born out of real-life galley scrambles, late-night salad cravings, and a deep belief that home cooking shouldn't be intimidating. It should be fun, freeing, and full of delicious surprises. Like you tossing together a vinaigrette and thinking, *"Wait... did I just make that?!"* (Spoiler: Yes. Yes you did.)

This isn't a "follow this perfectly or else" kind of cookbook. It's more like me sliding into your kitchen with a grin, handing you a spoon, and saying, "Let's play." Because flavor? It's personal. And learning to trust your taste buds? That's a whole vibe — one I want to help you rock.

So grab a jar, a few ingredients, and a little curiosity. The kitchen is yours now.

Let's shake things up — together.

With flavor love,

Inspiring Praise from Beyond the Apron

"From one salad lover to another! Kerstin Decook brings the heart of transformation into the kitchen—proving that even making a simple salad dressing can spark creativity, confidence, and joy. With her inspiring and uplifting voice, she encourages readers to trust their taste and create something amazing—guided by flavor, not formulas. This book is as empowering as it is delicious."

— Christine Kloser, *Award-Winning Publisher & Transformational Leader*

"Kerstin hands you the keys to flavor confidence—with sass, science, and a spoonful of adventure, she makes salad dressings wildly entertaining and unexpectedly empowering. Get ready to grab bigger bowls—once you start dressing like this, there's no going back."

— Ellen Contreras, *Host of Treasure Coast Connector*

"Kerstin's blueprints for salad dressings encourage you to taste, tweak, and trust yourself—turning everyday ingredients into something delicious. It's the kind of book that makes you feel capable, creative, and genuinely excited to get in the kitchen."

— Keren Kilgore, *Self-Mastery Coach & Publisher, Quantum Shift Media*

"A must-have for any home cook ready to ditch the bottled stuff and elevate their salad game—it's real food made simply, and with style."

— Sherri Mraz, *Health Coach & Founder of the Wellness Cooking Academy*

Praise from Real Home Cooks

I invited my three closest friends to Kerstin's *Dress to Impress* event, and we were all absolutely mesmerized. So many creative and fun ideas! Kerstin shares firsthand ways to add pizzazz to your salads. Her international education and deep cooking experience shine through, delivering impressive and captivating results. We're already counting down to the premiere of her next adventure, *Sauces*! A standing ovation and heartfelt applause — a true culinary talent.

— Victoria Blake

Before taking Kerstin's Dress to Impress online workshop, I stuck to store-bought dressings and didn't realize how easy it could be to make my own. Now I'm experimenting with flavor combos and having fun in the kitchen like never before!

— Steffi Von Bargen

Kerstin's approach helped me completely rethink my relationship with salad dressings. Her workshop on salad dressings inspired me to branch out, get creative, and fall in love with making my own flavorful dressings from scratch.

— Karin Gronau

Captain, First Mate... and Wait, I'm the Chef?!

A few years ago my husband and I decided to offer adventure charters through the beautiful San Juan Islands in the Pacific Northwest and eventually all the way up to Alaska. While the idea sounded great, I was wondering who would be in charge of what. Sure, my hubby was the captain — check. And I was supposed to be "First Mate" — check. We had both cruised the islands for years, so I was used to handling lines, navigating, and all the boaty stuff.

But then came the big question: who's going to be the Chef de Cuisine?

Cue *the look* from my husband — you know, the one that silently says, "That's all you, sweets."

Great. Thanks very much. That title was now mine to hold.

Sure, I could cook. But I wasn't a chef. Not yet.

My husband was perfectly fine serving up spaghetti and meatballs, but I knew — deep down — that nobody books a five-star yacht experience hoping for a three-star dinner.

I needed to upgrade my game in the kitchen to wear my newly appointed title proudly.

That's when I went all in.

I studied culinary arts across the U.S., Canada, and Europe — spent a small fortune (worth every penny!) — and logged countless hours learning the real hows and whys of great cooking. It wasn't about memorizing recipes — it was about thinking like a chef. Why does a sauce need lemon juice? What makes flavors sing together? How do you turn basic ingredients into something that makes people moan with joy at the dinner table?

Let me tell you — it changed everything.

Cooking went from being a chore and a stressful guessing game to something I truly enjoy — a creative playground where I get to experiment, play with flavor, and feel proud of what I serve. These days, I have more fun in the kitchen than ever — and I feel totally in control, creative, and fired up every time I cook.

Ready to impress? Let's go.

Captain and First Mate in action — cruising the San Juan Islands, serving up sea breeze, fun adventures, and better-than-spaghetti-and-meatball dinners.

Chapter 1

The Salad Dressing Awakening

Why Salad Dressings?

Because learning to make your own dressing is one of the easiest, quickest, most empowering things you can do in your kitchen. Seriously — once you know the basic ingredients and how they work together, the possibilities are endless.

You can whip up:

- A zippy vinaigrette for your lunch bowl
- A creamy, dreamy ranch for dipping veggies (or fries — no judgment)
- A honey-mustard drizzle so good it makes you look like a total pro

Salad dressings are where flavor begins. They teach you balance, texture, technique — and they're way easier to master than soufflés or seven-layer cakes. Plus, once you get the hang of it, you'll never buy another bottle of mystery goo again. Pinky promise.

This book is for every home cook who's ever:

- Bought "zesty Italian" only to find it tastes like disappointment
- Felt intimidated by fancy recipes with 27 ingredients
- Wanted to be more creative in the kitchen but didn't know where to start

- ♡ Tried to eat healthier but got stuck in a store-bought-dressing rut

- ♡ Felt bored doing the same ol' kitchen routine and craved something fresh and fun

- ♡ Wished they could whip up something impressive without a culinary degree

- ♡ Wanted to ditch the recipe-following training wheels and trust their own taste

You're in the right place, my friend. I'm here to help you unravel the secrets, master the magic formula, and finally have fun with food again.

By the time you're done with this book, you'll know exactly how to shake, whisk, and taste your way to salad dressings that are bright, bold, creamy, tangy, herby, spicy, or sweet — whatever your salad-loving heart desires.

And the best part? You don't need fancy tools or culinary training. Just a few ingredients, a little curiosity, and the willingness to taste and try.

Most importantly — you're not just improving your salad; you're stepping into a whole new level of cooking confidence. The kind that spills over into other parts of your kitchen (and your life).

So let's go.

Your bottle of ranch is officially on notice.

What's the point of salad dressing anyway?

Simple: to flavor, moisten, and upgrade your greens from "meh" to "more please." It's the magic that makes a salad feel like a dish, not a diet.

But let's be real: most bottled dressings? Total imposters. They talk a big game — creamy! zesty! gourmet! — but show up with a suitcase full of preservatives, sugar bombs, weird thickeners, and a whole lotta blah. What they *don't* bring? Freshness, zing, or anything that makes your taste buds dance.

I used to buy them too — mostly the creamy ones — and "tolerated" them because I didn't know how easy it was to make my own. Sure, I knew how to shake up a simple vinaigrette (thanks to my mom, who taught me the basics): olive oil, a splash of balsamic, a spoonful of mustard, and a bit of honey. It tasted fresh and yummy… until it got boring. Same-o same-o.

But when I dove into culinary school and learned the simple methods and flavor-building techniques for creating my own salad dressings, everything changed. These dressings weren't just fresher — they were brighter, balanced, and bursting with possibility. And the best part? They were fast and easy to whip up. Total game changer.

That was my lightbulb moment. Suddenly, I wasn't just making salad dressings… I was experimenting, tweaking, and playing with flavor. I wasn't following recipes — I was trusting my own taste buds.

That's exactly what I want for you.

Not to just follow my lead, but to build your own kitchen swagger — your style, your go-to formulas, your "oh wow, I made that?" kind of moments.

Ready? Let's move on.

Chapter 2

The Quartet That Rules Them All

Creating a memorable salad dressing hinges on mastering four key components: **Oil, Acid, Yum, and Fat**. Get these right, and you're on your way to dressing nirvana.

Let's break down what each one does — and how to start thinking like a flavor builder, not a recipe follower.

Since we're talking about how to *Dress to Impress (Your Salad, That Is!)* with a yummy sauce, we'll focus on the oils, acids, Yums, and fats that actually make sense in a dressing. Sure, there are a zillion ingredients that could technically fit each category — but we're sticking with the stars of the salad sauce show. Let's go.

Oil   Yum   Acid   Fat

 Oil: The Smooth Operator

What It Does:

Oil forms the base of most dressings, providing that silky, clingy texture that makes your greens glisten. It's the foundation that carries flavor, builds richness, and basically makes your salad feel like it just got promoted to main character status.

Now, you might be wondering: with so many oils out there, what's best for salad dressings?

Don't worry — I've got you: Here's your quick and flavorful guide to some of the most common oils and why (or why not) they deserve a spot in your dressing rotation.

Vegetable Oil: Super neutral and super processed. Budget-friendly, sure, but there's not much flavor or nutrition happening here. Use it if you must, but don't expect fireworks in your salad bowl.

Sunflower Oil: Mild, light, and vitamin E-rich. Great for simple vinaigrettes where you want the acid or herbs to shine — not the oil.

Canola Oil: Inexpensive and mild with a bit of buttery smoothness. Not fancy, but it plays nice with almost everything. It's also highly processed, so if you're aiming for a cleaner pantry, you might want to keep it in the occasional-use category. Still, it's a solid choice when you want your Yum ingredients to do the talking.

Soybean Oil: Often hiding in "vegetable oil" bottles. It's neutral but very processed and not super flavorful. More common in store-bought dressings than in fabulous homemade creations.

Corn Oil: Mild, slightly sweet, and totally workable if that's what you've got on hand. But don't expect it to win any flavor contests.

Sesame Oil: Toasted sesame oil = liquid gold. Deep, nutty, and bold. Just a few drops transform your dressing into a flavor bomb — especially for Asian-inspired dishes.

Peanut Oil: Light with a subtle nutty edge. Great for cooking and amazing if you're making a spicy peanut dressing. Not a go-to for most vinaigrettes, but it shines in the right context.

Olive Oil: The classic — and my favorite. Extra virgin olive oil (the good stuff) is fruity, peppery, and full of heart-healthy fats and antioxidants. It's made for dressings.

Grapeseed Oil: Light and neutral with just a hint of nuttiness. It lets the other flavors do their thing. A quiet team player in the salad world.

Avocado Oil: Creamy, mellow, and packed with healthy fats. It's like olive oil's chill cousin who brings good vibes and zero drama.

Nut Oils (Walnut, Pecan, etc.): Fancy, fragile, and full of flavor. A little goes a long way. Perfect for dressings, not for heat. Keep 'em cold and classy.

Each oil brings something different to the table — whether it's bold flavor, creamy texture, or budget-friendliness. Some (like corn, soy, canola or vegetable oil) are more processed and lower on the nutrient scale. Others, like extra virgin olive or avocado oil, offer more health perks and flavor depth.

That said — no judgment here. We all have different pocketbooks, flavor preferences, and pantry setups. Personally? I'm an extra virgin olive oil girl through and through — not just because of its richness, health benefits, and versatility, but also because I'm European, and olive oil basically runs in our veins. It's the go-to flavor booster over there, and I brought that love with me.

But hey — if another oil speaks to you or fits your vibe better? Go for it. It's your kitchen and your taste buds!

Since people always ask what olive oil is best to use, let's take a quick peek at those labels and clear up the mystery, my friend.

Understanding Olive Oil Labels (Without the Extra Virgin Drama)

When it comes to salad dressings, extra virgin olive oil (EVOO) is the gold standard — rich, flavorful, and packed with heart-healthy fats and antioxidants. It's made without heat or chemicals, which means you get all the good stuff (flavor and nutrients included). You might see terms like "first cold pressed" or "cold extraction" on the label — don't stress. These just mean the oil was made without heat, which is already true of any legit EVOO. "First cold pressed" is more of a marketing throwback, while "cold extraction" is the modern version using fancy machines instead of old-school presses.

The key to picking a great EVOO? Look for dark glass bottles, quality seals (like PDO, COOC, or USDA Organic), and harvest or best-by dates to ensure freshness. And always trust your taste buds — a real EVOO should smell vibrant and maybe give a little peppery kick. That's not a flaw — that's flavor power.

Now that we've got the oil sorted, let's look at the next key component that brings balance and brightness to the salad sauce party.

 # Acid: The Zesty Sidekick

What It Does:

Acid is your salad's wake-up call — the zinger, the sharp-tongued flavor hero that cuts through the fat and brings everything to life. Forget to invite acid to the party, and your dressing's just oil in a fancy outfit with no personality.

Tangy Options:

Vinegars: Balsamic, red wine, white wine, apple cider, rice vinegar, sherry vinegar, malt vinegar, champagne vinegar, coconut vinegar — and even fruit-infused vinegars like blueberry, raspberry or fig. The variety lets you mix things up and create bold, unexpected flavor combos.

Citrus Juices: Lemon, lime, orange, or grapefruit juice bring a fresh, fruity punch that brightens every bite.

Fresh Fruit — yes, really! —like tangy berries like raspberries, blackberries, or even strawberries can be mashed and whisked right into a vinaigrette for a naturally sweet-tart twist. Tropical fruits like pineapple or mango can also bring bright acidity and a sunny vibe to your dressing. Just remember to taste as you go and balance that sweetness with a splash of vinegar or citrus if needed.

 Yum: The Flavor Bombs

What It Does:

This is where you get to play and personalize your dressing. Yum ingredients add depth, complexity, and character. Because without Yum? Your dressing's got no spark, no sass, and definitely no reason to show up on your salad. This is where the magic happens, baby.

Flavor Boosters:

Mustard: Adds spice and helps emulsify (bind) the dressing.

Garlic & Shallots: Offer a pungent kick and aromatic allure.

Herbs & Spices: Think basil, oregano, thyme, or even a pinch of chili flakes.

Sweeteners: A touch of honey, maple syrup, or agave can balance acidity.

Chiles: Introduce heat and a spicy dimension to your dressing.

Fermented Sauces (Fish/Soy Sauce, Worcestershire): Add umami depth and a savory complexity.

And last but not least, the fourth component:

 # Fat: The Creamy Dream

What It Does:

Fat brings the richness, the body, and that luscious, velvety texture that makes creamy dressings totally irresistible. Unlike vinaigrettes — which lean on oil — creamy dressings start with the fat front and center, like mayo, yogurt, or sour cream, giving you smooth satisfaction right out of the gate.

Hang tight — more flavor magic coming your way, including when to bust out the fat and when to let oil do the heavy lifting.

Creamy Add-Ins:

Yogurt or Sour Cream: Bring tang and creaminess.

Buttermilk: Light, tangy, and perfect for thinning out thicker dressings while keeping that creamy texture.

Crème fraîche: Rich and velvety with a slight tang — fancy but totally approachable.

Mayonnaise: Adds a smooth, velvety texture.

Avocado: For a dairy-free creamy option with a health boost.

Peanut Butter: A creamy, nutty powerhouse — especially in Asian-inspired dressings. (Try it with lime juice, garlic, and a splash of soy sauce for magic in a bowl.)

Tahini: Smooth, earthy, and slightly bitter — made from sesame seeds and a star player in Mediterranean and Middle Eastern-style dressings. Think lemon-tahini bliss with a little garlic and water to thin it out.

Mixing It Up: Your Dressing, Your Rules

With these four components, you're ready to experiment and whip up dressings that hit your flavor sweet spot. But here's a little flavor wisdom to keep in your back pocket:

There are two kinds of salad sauce personalities — the light, flirty vinaigrettes and the rich, creamy showstoppers — and the difference is all in the makings.

- ⇒ **Lighter vinaigrettes** are made with **Oil + Acid + Yum** — smooth, zesty, and oh-so-flexible.

- ⇒ **Richer, creamy dressings** are made with **Fat + Acid + Yum** — velvety, satisfying, and just as easy to riff on.

This tiny twist in your base formula changes the whole game — and knowing it? Total kitchen flex.

Curious how to put it all into action? Don't worry, my friend — we'll dive deeper into both formulas in Chapter 4 where the real flavor-building fun begins.

And just one more thing to sprinkle on top: even the most fabulous formula can flop if your ingredients are past their prime. And with raw creations like salad dressings, you can't just cook the life back into limp lemons or sad herbs.

So grab the good stuff — fresh lemon juice (not that reconstituted stuff in the bottle), vibrant herbs (no wilted wallflowers), and ingredients that haven't been clinging to the back of your fridge since last month. Your salad — and your taste buds — deserve VIP treatment, not a pity party.

Vinaigrettes & Dressings

Oil

Acid

Fat

Yum

Oil	Acid	Fat	Yum
Olive Oil, Avocado Oil, Vegetable Oil, Nut Oil, Sesame Oil, Flavord Oil	Vinegar (*Red, White, Balsamic, Rice, Sherry*), Citrus (*Lemon, Lime, Orange*)	Mayo, Yogurt, Creme Fraiche, Sour Creme, Buttermilk	Mustard, Garlic, Shallots, Spices, Herbs, Zest, Honey, Sugar, Chiles, Fermented (*Fish/Soya Sauce*)

Vinaigrettes

Dressings

Before we roll into the next chapter — where we dive into the silky science behind what makes salad sauces sing — let me show you what's always hanging out in my fridge.

Because let's be honest — when you're a salad fanatic (hi, it's me), having the right ingredients on hand is *everything*.

Here's my go-to salad-lover's fridge stash for whipping up vinaigrettes and dressings in no time flat:

   Plain Greek yogurt, sour cream, mayo, and mustard –
       my creamy crew.

   Fresh lemons or limes, garlic, and shallots – bright, zippy, and always
       on call.

   Honey in the pantry and salt + pepper by the stove – sweet, salty,
       perfect.

   And of course, the **oh-so-delicious EVOO** – never not stocked.

With these in reach, I can whip up something fresh and flavorful on the fly — then just toss in whatever else is hanging out in the kitchen that day. That's the magic of knowing your flavor formula: no recipes, no panic, just pure, saucy freedom.

Now, it's time to explore the hidden secret behind truly vibrant, flavorful salad dressings. We're about to enter the magical world of emulsions!

Chapter 3

Emulsions – The Secret to Creamy, Dreamy Dressings

Let's talk about the silky science behind a great dressing — emulsion.

Understanding emulsions is like learning kitchen magic. It's how you turn oil and acid (which is water-based) — two liquids that normally repel each other — into a creamy, dreamy dressing.

In the culinary world, emulsions are considered an essential cooking technique and the secret to vibrant and flavorful sauces and dressings.

Let's break down the three main types:

Types of Emulsions

Temporary Emulsion: Shake oil and water-based acid together and you'll see a quick emulsion form — the water molecules break up the oil into tiny droplets until it is hard to recognize what's oil and what's water. But give it time, and they'll split up again (classic) — see illustration

Semi-Permanent Emulsion: Add something like mustard or honey to the mix (which act as mild emulsifiers), and the oil and acid will stay friends a bit longer — not forever, but long enough to dress your salad without drama.

Permanent Emulsion: A permanent emulsion is one where oil and acid stay bonded together with the help of a powerful emulsifier — like egg yolk. Thanks to its lecithin content, egg yolk is a rock star in sauces like aioli or hollandaise. But let's be real: we're not cracking raw eggs straight into our salad dressings.

Instead, we use mayo — which is already a glorious emulsion made from egg yolk, oil, and either vinegar or lemon juice. It's not an emulsifier itself, but it's a fabulous pre-blended shortcut to creamy, stable dressings that won't ghost your salad halfway through dinner.

The one thing you *really* need to remember?

The stronger the emulsifier, the longer the emulsion holds.

Later, I'll show you exactly how to make mayo from scratch — and you'll see for yourself how a permanent emulsion comes together in all its rich, creamy glory.

So what actually glues all this silky magic together? Let me break it down the *Kerstin* way (science lovers, take a deep breath):

An emulsifier is like a charming party host — one side flirts with water (aka the acid), the other cozies up to oil. It brings them together, gets them mingling, and before you know it, everyone's dancing in a smooth, dreamy blend that doesn't split up halfway through the night.

Pretty cool, right?

Emulsions

The Secret to Vibrant and Flavorful Sauces and Dressings

Emulsion = Mixture of Two Unmixable Liquids

• Temporary   • Semi-Permanent   • Permanent

Oil

Acid

→ Shake / Whisk →

→ Leave alone for 1 hour →

=Temporary Emulsion (Vinaigrette)

Oil
Egg yolk
Acid

→ Whisk / Blend →

→ Fully Blended →

=Permanent Emulsion (Mayonnaise)

The Emulsifier Lineup: Your Kitchen MVPs

Now that you know *what* emulsions are and *why* they matter, let's talk tools. Not whisks and blenders — I mean the behind-the-scenes heroes that actually make the magic happen.

Emulsifiers come in all kinds of forms — plant-based, animal-based, and even synthetic ones (hello, xanthan gum). But don't worry, we're keeping it real here. No need to raid a science lab — just your pantry.

You already know egg yolk is a heavy hitter (hello, homemade mayo magic). But when it comes to everyday salad dressings, it's the pantry MVPs — like **mustard, honey, tomato paste, ketchup, miso, and garlic paste** — that do the daily heavy lifting. They're gentler and not quite as mighty as lecithin, but they hold their own in the home cook's kitchen.

Toss a little mustard and honey into your vinaigrette, and boom — you've got yourself a semi-permanent emulsion. It'll hold longer than plain oil and vinegar, but if it starts to split? No biggie. Just shake, whisk, or blend that baby back to life.

My Favorite Emulsion Truth: Let's not overcomplicate things.
Put your ingredients in a bowl or jar, stir or shake them like you're making magic — and watch it come together. That's the power of understanding how your ingredients work together.

Since mayo is the queen bee of permanent emulsions, and a total game-changer once people try making it themselves, let's dive into the art of making homemade mayonnaise that puts store-bought blabbery stuff to shame.

Emulsifier MVPs

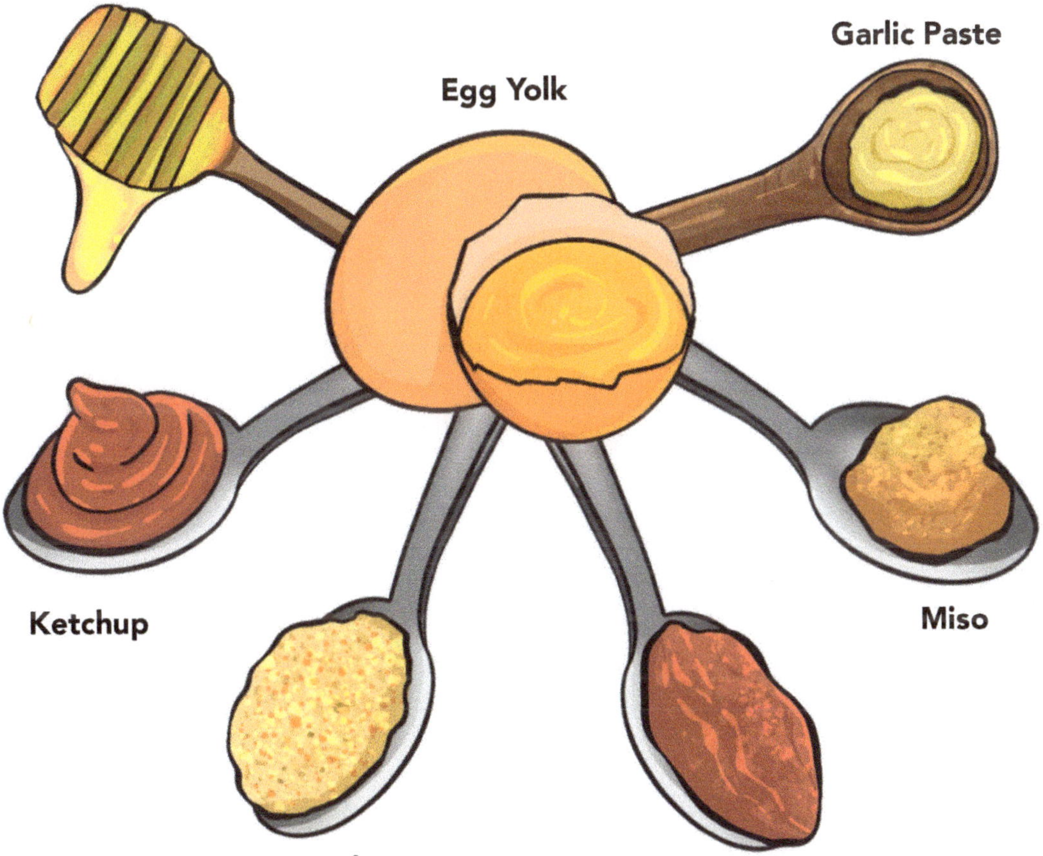

Honey

Egg Yolk

Garlic Paste

Ketchup

Miso

Mustard

Tomato Paste

Blender Royalty: The Creamiest Mayo on the Block

Let's be real: once you've made mayo from scratch, your taste buds will stage a protest if you ever go back to the jarred stuff. It's creamier, fresher, tangier, and just plain better.

And the best part? It takes under a minute with one tool and zero drama.

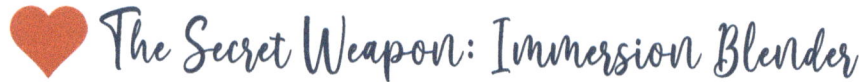 The Secret Weapon: Immersion Blender

That's right. We're skipping the slow oil drizzle nonsense.
Grab your immersion blender and a blender cup — and let the flavor vortex begin.

If You're Not Familiar with an Immersion Blender, Let's Change That.

An immersion blender (sometimes called a hand blender or stick blender) is your secret weapon for homemade dressings. Instead of slowly drizzling oil into a bowl while whisking like a maniac, you simply immerse the blades into your ingredients (yup, that's where the name comes from) and let it work its vortex magic — pulling everything together into creamy, dreamy perfection. It's compact, quick, and perfect for whipping up small-batch wonders like dressings, dips, or even soups.

Heads Up: Make sure you use the blender cup that came with it — or any tall container that's just a little wider than the blades. If you try this in a giant bowl, the vortex will fizzle out faster than a bad first date. Small and snug = creamy success!

What You'll Need:

1 room temperature egg (yes, the whole thing — yolk and white!)

1 tsp Dijon mustard

1 tbsp vinegar or lemon juice

2/3 cup neutral oil (Olive oil can be too strong and make your mayo slightly bitter)

Pinch of salt

Optional: a splash of water if it gets too thick

Why the *whole* egg?

Most classic mayo recipes call for just the yolk — because that's where the emulsifying magic happens (thanks, lecithin!). But I like to throw in the whole egg. Why? Because egg whites are mostly water, and mayo often needs a touch of water to loosen it up anyway. Plus, using the whole egg adds lightness to the texture and makes the process extra foolproof. Win-win!

But Wait — What About the Raw Egg?

Let's talk about it.

Yes, you're using a raw egg. And yes, some people worry about salmonella. Here's the deal: I've cooked with raw eggs my entire life — including in Germany, where we even eat raw beef (hello, Mettbrötchen!) — and I've never gotten sick.

The secret? Use the freshest, highest-quality eggs you can find. Look for pasture-raised eggs from trusted local sources or farms.

Still unsure? You can always use pasteurized eggs from the store — they're heat-treated to reduce risk but still raw enough to work beautifully in recipes like this.

Bottom line? Your kitchen, your comfort level — you call the shots.

And hey, if making mayo from scratch isn't your thing right now? No judgment whatsoever. Just skip ahead to Chapter 4 and keep rocking your store-bought favorite.

But... if you're even the tiniest bit curious, let me show you how quick and magical it is to whip up your own creamy mayo goodness at home.

Let's do this.

How to Make It (The Kerstin Way – the best and fastest way, in my humble opinion)

1. **Add ALL ingredients to the blender cup.** No slow streams, no multitasking — just dump and go.

   Heads-up on oil ratio: One *egg yolk* can emulsify up to about 2/3 cup of oil. That's your magic number. Even though we're using the whole egg (for reasons above), this yolk-to-oil ratio still matters. Go beyond it, and your emulsion may break or never thicken. Stick to it, and you're golden.

2. **Place your immersion blender all the way to the bottom of the cup.** Make sure it's snug and centered — the cup should be just slightly wider than your blender head.

3. **Press the button and let the vortex do its thing.** You'll watch it emulsify from the bottom up. It's kitchen magic, and it never gets old.

4. **Once it starts looking creamy, slowly lift the blender upward to blend the rest.**

5. **Taste and tweak as needed:**
   - More lemon for zip
   - More salt for balance
   - A touch more Dijon for sass

Boom. Mayo. Made by YOU.

Store in a sealed jar in the fridge for 3–4 days.

Flavor It Up: Once you've nailed the base, go wild:
   - Garlic mayo
   - Chipotle mayo
   - Lemon herb
   - Basil, dill, or parsley
   - Sundried tomato
   - Horseradish or curry

Use it in creamy dressings, sandwich spreads, dipping sauces — or eat it by the spoon (no judgment).

Your Turn!

You've read the magic — now it's time to whip it into reality. Rally your ingredients, grab your blender cup, and fire up that flavor vortex! Whip it, taste it, tweak it — and when that creamy goodness appears, own it like the kitchen rockstar you are.

Welcome to homemade mayo greatness — and welcome to the permanent emulsion elite.

Chapter 4

The Magic Formula

(And Why Chefs Don't Follow the Old Rules)

Ever heard the phrase "3 parts oil to 1 part acid"? It's the old-school vinaigrette rule — and sure, it works... but today, we're tossing the rulebook out the window and making way for full-on flavor freedom.

The 3:1 ratio? It's a nice starting point — but dressings should match your taste buds, not a ratio.

Understanding the Classic Ratio

The traditional 3:1 ratio offers a balanced starting point:

Three parts oil to one part acid creates a harmonious blend that suits many palates.

But here's the thing — everyone's taste buds are different, and the "perfect" balance can vary depending on your preferences and the specific ingredients you're working with.

>   Like a sharper, more tangy vinaigrette? **Use less oil**, closer to a **2:1 ratio**.

>   Prefer a milder, softer flavor? **Use more oil**, around a **4:1 ratio** to
>   mellow out the acidity.

The key is to **taste and adjust** — making sure your dressing enhances the flavor of your salad and makes your taste buds sing.

Crafting Your Signature Dressing

We are going to break this down into two parts: Light Vinaigrettes and Richer, Creamier Dressings. First up — the light and zesty kind.

Part 1: Light Vinaigrettes – *The Gateway to Dressing Glory*

Let's start with the easiest, most flexible foundation: a Basic Vinaigrette.

This simple but powerful trio — Oil + Acid + Yum — is my favorite way to kick things off, and the perfect launchpad for building real flavor confidence.

Here's how I teach it in my class: keep two components the same (oil and Yum), and change just one — the acid.

Why do we keep the oil and Yums the same? So you can really taste the difference each acid makes — it's like a flavor boot camp for your taste buds!

It's one of the fastest ways to sharpen your instincts and grow serious kitchen swagger. Once you've built that foundation, you can start blinging up your vinaigrettes with all kinds of extra Yums and fancy oils.

But for now? Keep it basic and let the flavor learning begin.

The Base Formula – We Need an Oil, an Acid, and Some Basic Yum

Oil: Pick one (you know which one is my fave)

Yums (Flavor Boosters): My go-to base combo:
- Dijon mustard
- Honey or agave
- Salt and pepper

Acid Swap Ideas:

- White wine vinegar
- Red wine vinegar
- Apple cider vinegar
- Balsamic glaze
- Champagne vinegar
- Lemon juice (or whatever citrus you love)

Or honestly… whatever makes your lips pucker and your taste buds perk up when you find it in your pantry!

Need a Starting Point?

Wondering, "How much oil do I even use?"

Start with about ¼ **cup of oil** as your foundation. Add **2–3 teaspoons of acid**, and a **small dollop or pinch of each Yum** you're using (*think: a teaspoonful for a dollop, a pinch for tiny things like minced garlic or spices — keep it light and playful*).

That'll make enough for **2–4 salads** — not too much, not too little, and perfect for playing around.

You can always add more Yum, but once it's in, you can't take it out — that's why it's so important to mix, taste, and adjust as you go.

Taste Like a Pro: Instead of just tasting from a spoon, dip a salad leaf or a cucumber slice into your vinaigrette — it'll give you a much better sense of how the flavors will actually play out on your salad.

Your vinaigrette, your rules — just give it a little love along the way.

Your Flavor Adventure Awaits...

Coming up are some of my favorite vinaigrettes you can whisk together using this method. No strict measurements — just a handful of tasty ingredients and your inner chef guiding the way.

Use these as inspiration. Mix, match, taste, and tweak. You're not following a recipe anymore — you're creating.

And hey — if your flavor preferences are a little different than mine? Awesome. That's the whole point.

Just grab a vinaigrette recipe you love and break it down:
- What's the oil?
- What's the acid?
- What are the Yums (your flavor boosters)?

Boom — you've cracked the code.

Use the blank illustration page to jot down *your* favorite combos. Then? Go wild. Make it yours.

For example: Want a Greek-style vinaigrette? Here's a flavor-forward idea:
- **Oil:** Olive oil
- **Acid:** Red wine vinegar
- **Yums:** Garlic, oregano, Dijon mustard, salt & pepper

Like it tangier? Add more vinegar. Love garlic? Load it up. Prefer it mellow? Dial it back. No garlic? No problem. You do YOU.

Want a Honey-Mustard Lemon Vinaigrette? Try this combo:

- **Oil:** Olive oil
- **Acid:** Fresh lemon juice
- **Yums:** Honey, stone-ground mustard, fresh thyme, salt & pepper

Craving more zing? Add extra lemon juice. Want it a little sweeter? Drizzle in more honey. Feeling herby? Go wild with the thyme — or swap it out for basil or tarragon.

This is your dressing, your kitchen, your rules.

This is how you break free from rigid recipes — and walk boldly into the delicious world of flavor confidence.

Your Turn!

Grab your oil, pick your acid, toss in some Yum, and mix up your own vinaigrette magic.

Taste it, tweak it, and remember — no two vinaigrettes are ever exactly the same, and that's the best part.

Your salad's about to get a serious upgrade.

And remember, you don't need perfection - just a spoon and a sense of adventure.

5 Basic Vinaigrettes

Note: Add Other Yums and/or Oils to your liking.

Yum
Dijon Mustard,
Honey/Agave *(optional to offset the Acid)*,
Salt & Pepper

Acid
Any ONE of the following:
- White Wine Vinegar
- Red Wine Vinegar
- Apple Cider Vinegar
- Balsamic Vinegar/Glaze
- Champagne Vinegar

Oil
Olive Oil

Make or Shake in Jar

Italian Vinaigrette

Note: Fresh herbs are great too but it will shorten the shelf life. Another tip: Freeze in ice cube trays and use a few instead of butter or oil when cooking, it's already seasoned.

Yum
Dijon Mustard, Garlic,
Honey/Agave *(optional to offset the tangy flavors)*,
Salt & Pepper,
Italian Seasoning or Dried Herbs
(Parsley, Oregano or Thyme)

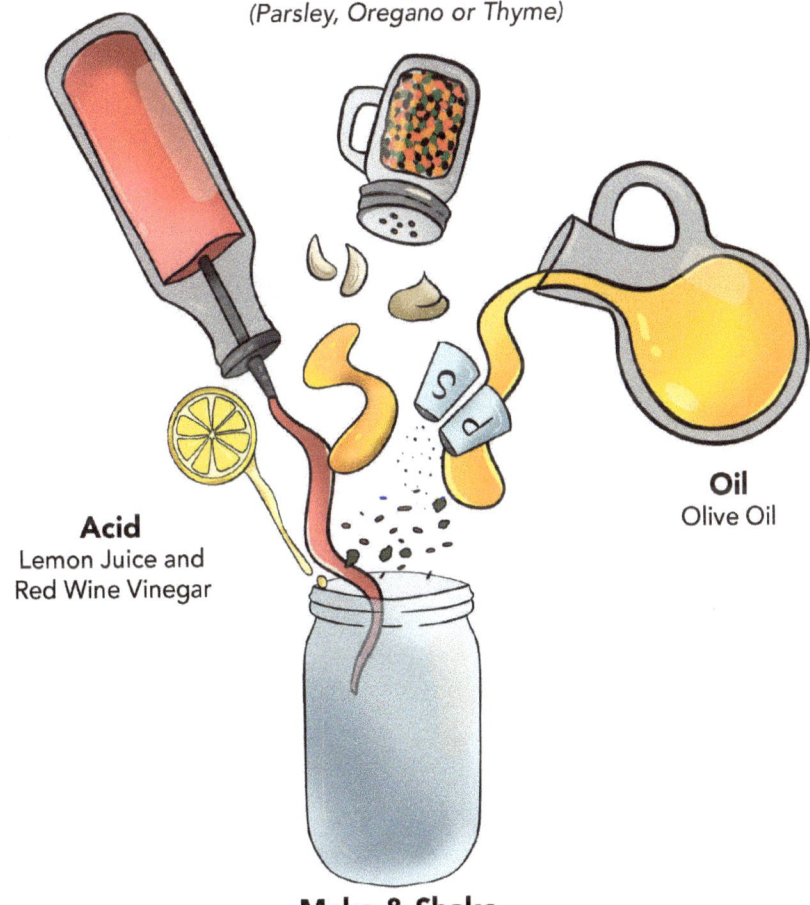

Acid
Lemon Juice and
Red Wine Vinegar

Oil
Olive Oil

Make & Shake

Citrus Vinaigrette

Note: Keep in fridge for up to 1 week *(in airtight container)*

Yum
Orange Zest,
Dijon Mustard,
Honey/Agave *(optional to offset the tangy flavors)*,
Salt & Pepper

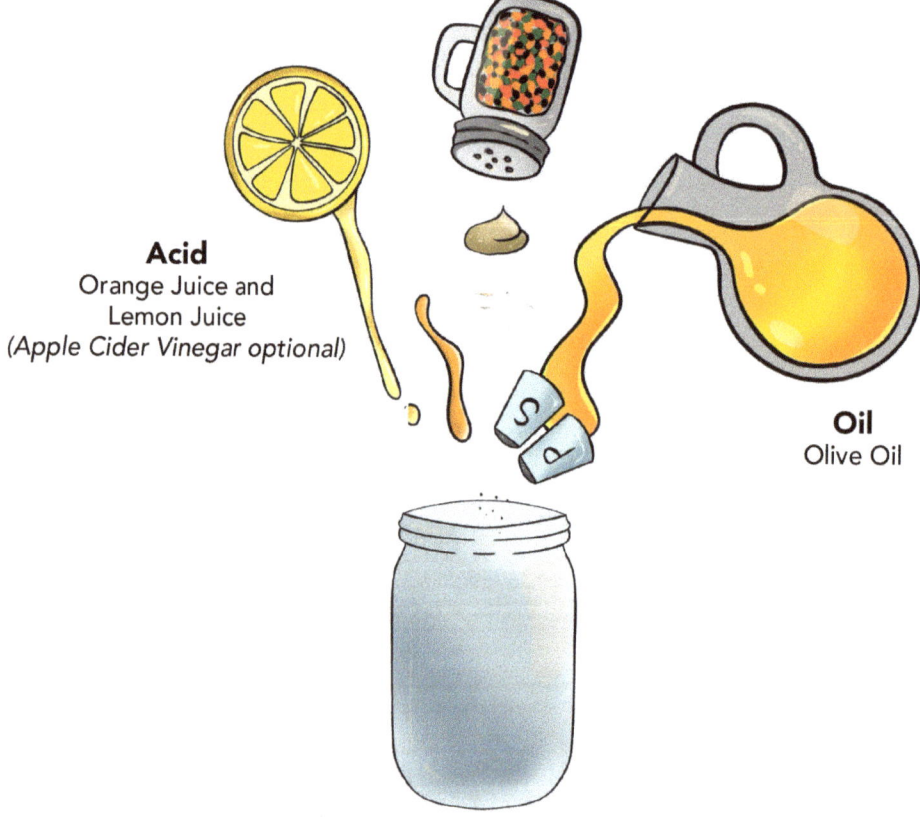

Acid
Orange Juice and
Lemon Juice
(Apple Cider Vinegar optional)

Oil
Olive Oil

Make & Shake in Jar

Cilantro Lime Vinaigrette

Note: For a creamy version, add Greek yogurt or avocado.
For a spicier version, add a bit of jalapeño.
Refrigerate in air-tight container & use within a few days.

YUM
Garlic *(for a little bite)*,
Honey/Agave *(optional to offset the tangy flavors)*,
Dijon Mustard,
Fresh Cilantro *(lots)*,
Salt
Ground Coriander *(optional but gives vinaigrette extra depth of flavor)*

Acid
Lime Juice and
White or Rice Wine Vinegar

Oil
Olive Oil

Use Immersion Blender
(or Food Processor)

Sesame Ginger Vinaigrette

Note: Because of fresh ingredients, keeps only for a few days in fridge.

Yum
Soy Sauce,
Garlic,
Honey/Agave *(optional to offset the tangy flavors)*,
Fresh Grated Ginger,
Sriracha *(optional for spicy kick)*,
Sesame Seeds,
Finely Chopped Scallion

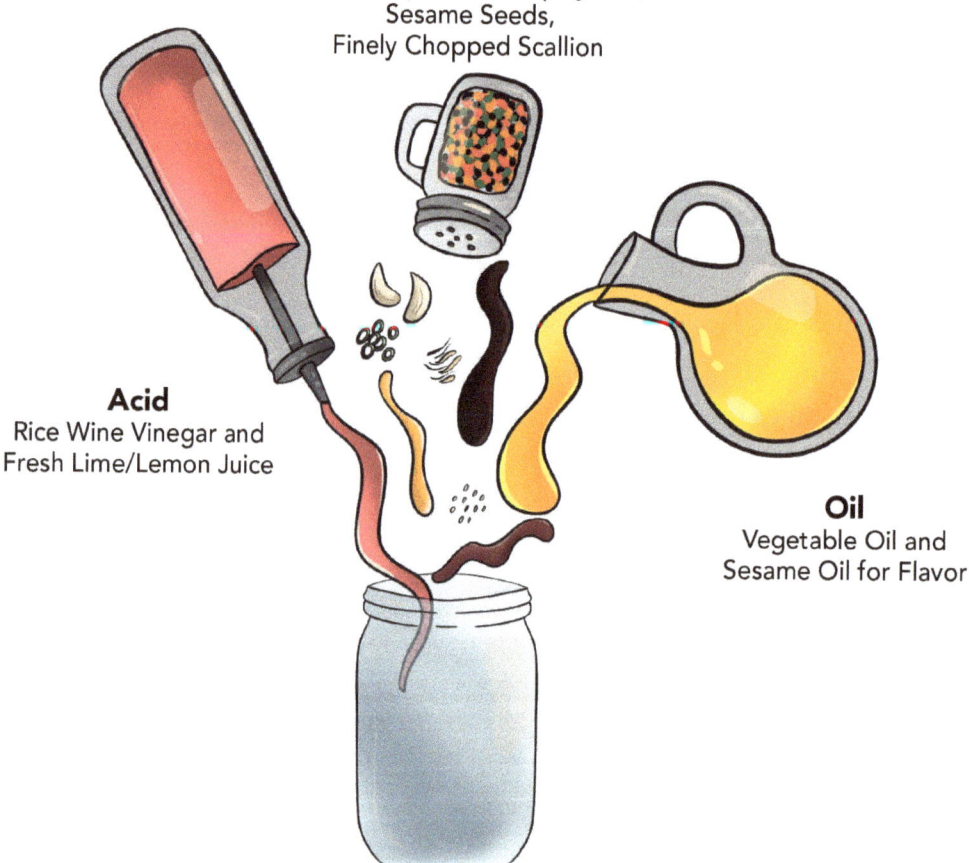

Acid
Rice Wine Vinegar and
Fresh Lime/Lemon Juice

Oil
Vegetable Oil and
Sesame Oil for Flavor

Make & Shake

46

Raspberry Vinaigrette

Note: It freezes well too.
Best used within one week.

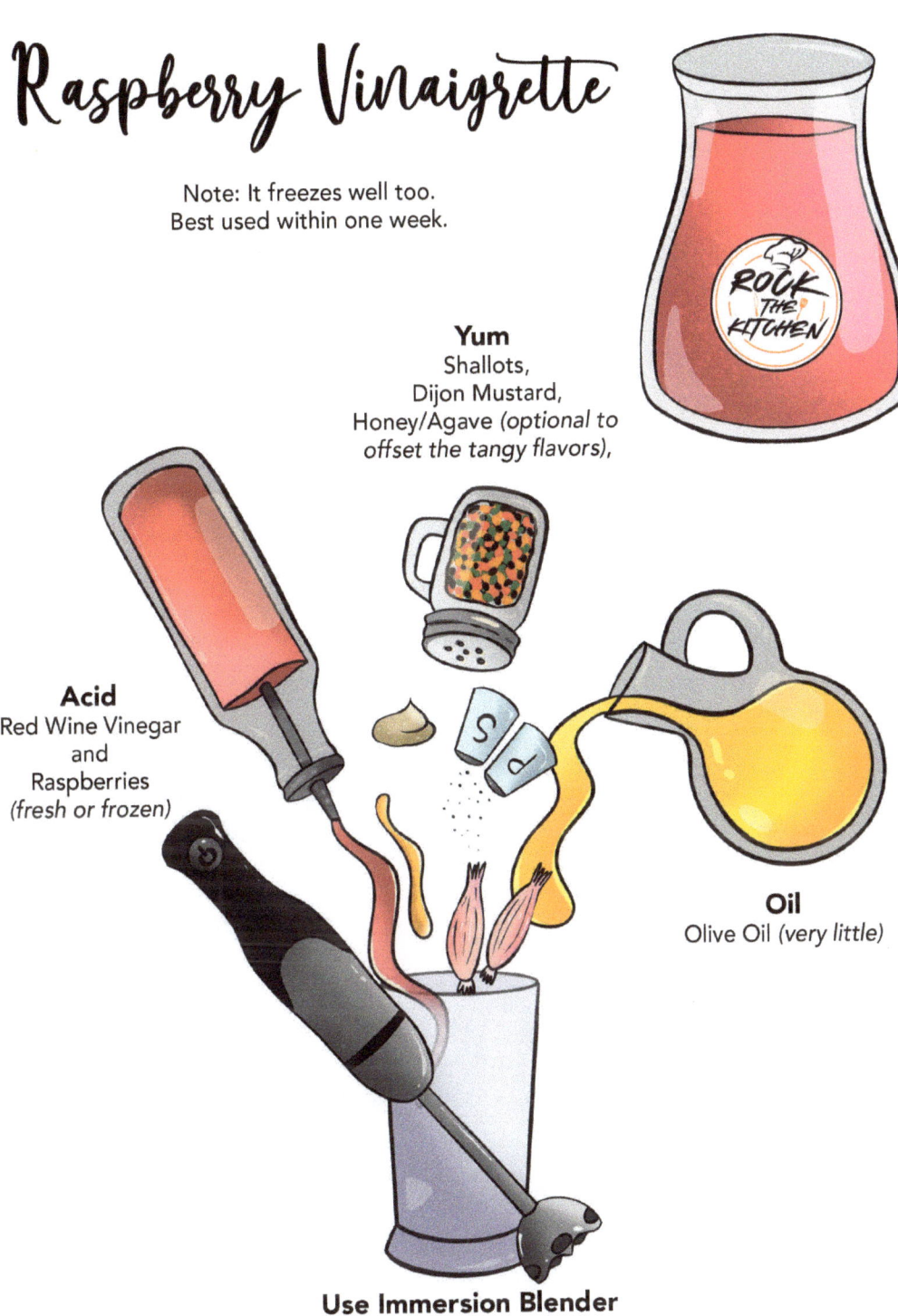

Yum
Shallots,
Dijon Mustard,
Honey/Agave *(optional to offset the tangy flavors)*,

Acid
Red Wine Vinegar
and
Raspberries
(fresh or frozen)

Oil
Olive Oil *(very little)*

Use Immersion Blender
(or Food Processor)

Create Your Signature Sauce

No Rules, Just Flavor

You've learned the formula — now it's your time to freestyle.
Let your fancy taste buds call the shots — jot down your custom combo below!

Name Your Creation _____

Part 2: Richer, Creamier Dressings – *When You Want It Smooth, Tangy & Totally Satisfying*

Now that you've got vinaigrettes under your belt (go, you!), it's time to dip into something a little more luscious: **creamy dressings**.

These babies are thicker, richer, and bring a whole new texture game to the table. Instead of oil as the star, they start with **fat** — think mayo, yogurt, or buttermilk — although oil sometimes sneaks back in to keep things extra silky.

Think ranch, Caesar, honey mustard… you know, the kind of dressings you want to slather on everything from salads to sandwiches to your finger. (No judgment.)

The Formula (Let's Clear Things Up)

First, let's talk formula — because this is different from the ratios we used with vinaigrettes.

The creamy dressing formula is simple and fabulous:

Fat + Acid + Yum

That's your base structure. But here's where it gets a little different...

We're *not* sticking to strict ratios like 3:1 or 2:1 anymore.

Why? Because creamy dressings can go from tasty to *face-puckering tangy* real fast if you add too much acid up front.

Pro Move:

Start with about ¼ cup of your **creamy base** (Fat). Add a **small splash of Acid** *(think: about 1 teaspoon — just enough acid to make your dressing dance, not cry)*. Then layer in your Yums slowly. Mix, taste, tweak, and adjust as you go. Boom — dressing magic.

Coming up are some of my Faves...

These aren't "recipes" in the traditional sense — they're *jumping-off points*, delicious blueprints for you to mix, match, and make your own.

Want more tang? Add a little lemon.
Too thick? Splash in a little water or buttermilk.
Need a flavor lift? Throw in something unexpected!

Want to lighten things up? Try combining fats — maybe a bit of mayo with a scoop of sour cream or a spoonful of plain yogurt. Creamy, balanced, and totally customizable. *That's* how your signature dressing is born.

And if you're using that homemade mayo from earlier? Boom — your creamy creation just got a serious upgrade in flavor and flair.

Your Turn!

Pick a creamy dressing from the list — or freestyle your own flavor bomb.

Start with a fat you love, splash in some acid, and sprinkle in the Yums until you're building boldness by the spoonful.

Taste, tweak, and layer like the kitchen rockstar you're becoming.

Ranch Dressing

Note: For lighter dressing swap sour cream for plain yogurt.
Chill for at least one hour to allow flavors to blend.
Should keep up to 2 weeks in fridge *(in sealed container)*

Yum
Dried Herbs *(Dill, Parsley, Chives)*,
Onion & Garlic Powder,
Salt & Pepper

Acid
Lemon Juice

Fat
Mayonnaise,
Sour Cream and
Buttermilk *(to taste & thin)*

Whisk in Bowl

Blue Cheese Dressing

Note: For lighter dressing, swap sour cream for plain yogurt. Chill for at least an hour to allow flavors to blend. Should keep up to 2 weeks in fridge *(in sealed container)*.

Yum
Crumbled Blue Cheese *(like Gorgonzola)*,
Parsley,
Salt & Pepper

Fat
Mayonnaise,
Sour Cream and
Buttermilk *(to taste & thin)*

Acid
Lemon Juice

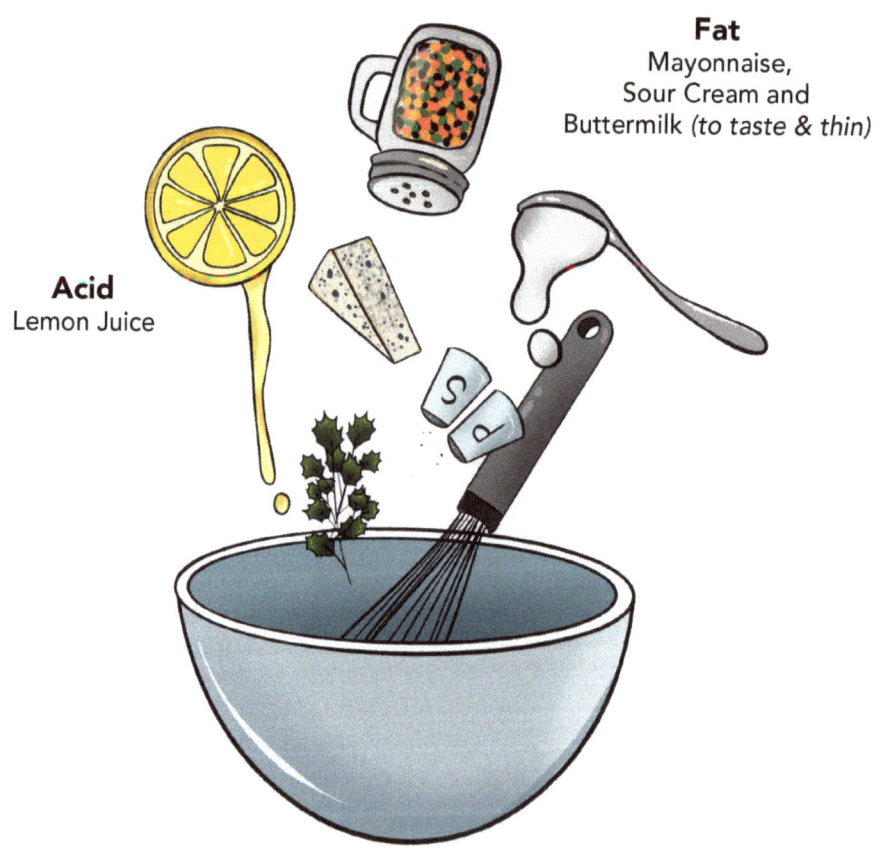

Whisk in Bowl

Caesar Dressing

Note: If the Anchovy flavor is too strong for your palate, you can leave them out and add a bit more Worchestershire *(an English version of Fish Sauce)*, yet the Anchovies give the dressing its captivating, savory flavor.

Yum
Garlic, Anchovy Filets or Paste, Dijon Mustard, Worcestershire, Freshly Grated Parmesan or Parmesan-Reggiano, Salt & Pepper

Acid
Fresh Lemon Juice

Fat
Mayonnaise,
Greek Yogurt *(optional)*

Use Immersion Blender
(or Food Processor)

Honey Mustard Dressing

Note: Chill for at least an hour to allow flavors to blend.
Keeps about 10 days in fridge *(in sealed container)*

Yum
Dijon or Ground Mustard,
Honey, Salt & Pepper
Minced Garlic *(for optional savory depth)*

Acid
Apple Cider Vinegar or
Fresh Lime/Lemon Juice

Fat
Mayonnaise

Whisk in Bowl

Thousand Island Dressing

Note: Chill for several hours and stir occasionally for sugar to dissolve and flavors to blend. Should keep in fridge for about one week *(in sealed container)*.

Yum
Ketchup,
Onion *(yellow or red)*,
Sugar, Sweet Pickle Relish,
Garlic *(optional)*, Tabasco *(optional)*,
Salt & Pepper

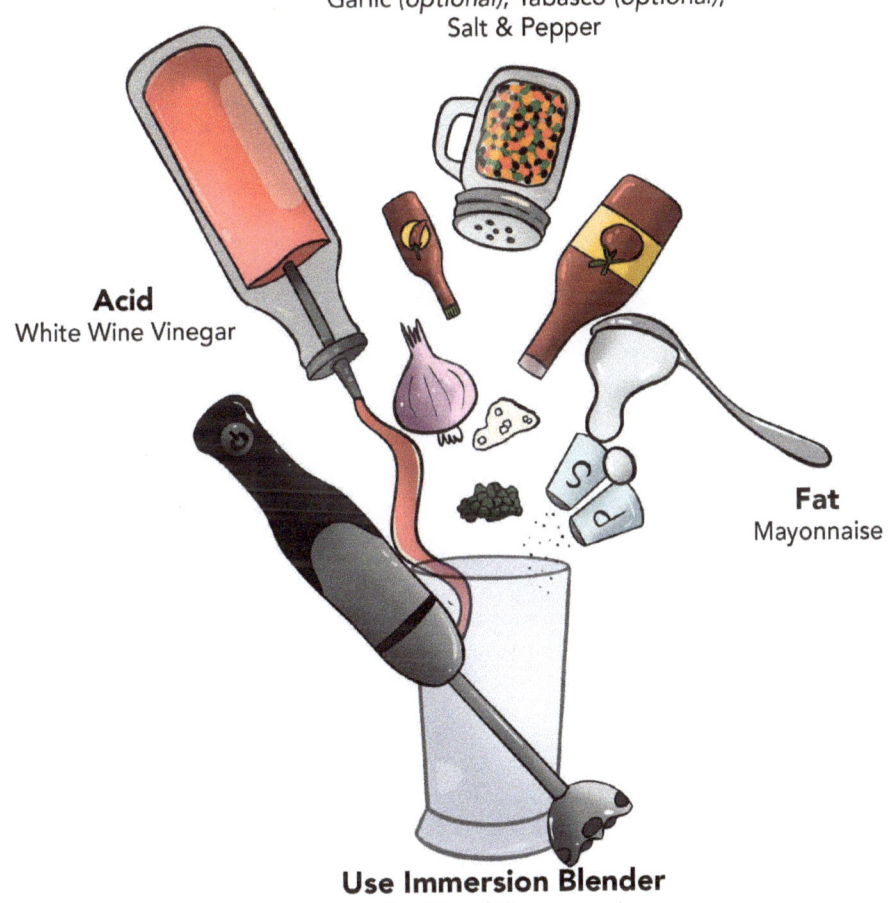

Acid
White Wine Vinegar

Fat
Mayonnaise

Use Immersion Blender
(or Food Processor)

Avocado-Cilantro Dressing

Note: Keeps in fridge for 3-4 days (*in airtight container*).

Yum
Cilantro,
Garlic,
Salt & Pepper,
(*optional: Olive Oil or Water to thin*)

Fat
Ripe Avocado,
Plain Yogurt and/or
Sour Cream

Acid
Lime Juice

Use Immersion Blender
(*or Food Processor*)

Creamy Poppy Seed Dressing

Note: For a lighter dressing, swap out the mayo for plain yogurt or use some of each. It will keep in the fridge for up to a week. Shake well before using.

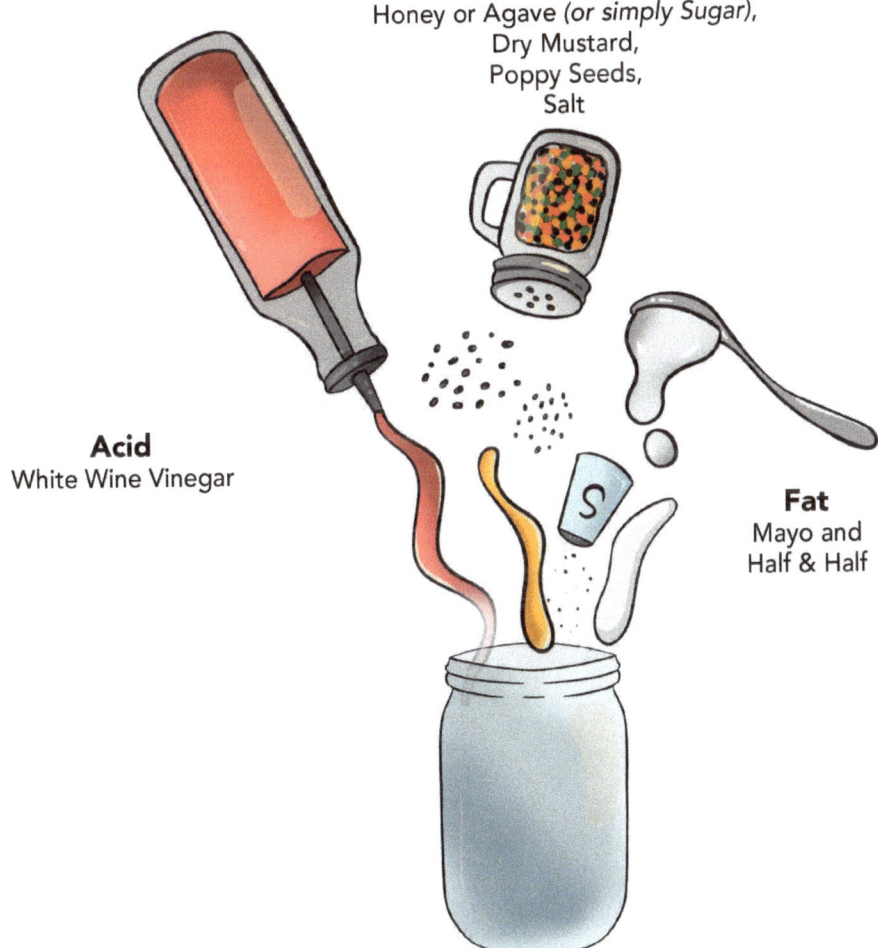

Yum
Honey or Agave *(or simply Sugar)*,
Dry Mustard,
Poppy Seeds,
Salt

Acid
White Wine Vinegar

Fat
Mayo and
Half & Half

Whisk or Shake in a Jar

Green Goddess Dressing

Note: For lighter dressing, swap out the mayo for plain yogurt or sour cream. This dressing will keep in the fridge for up to 3 days.

Yum
Garlic, Parsley, Cilantro, Chives, Tarragon or Basil, Salt & Pepper,
(Optional: Anchovy Paste or Fileted Anchovies)

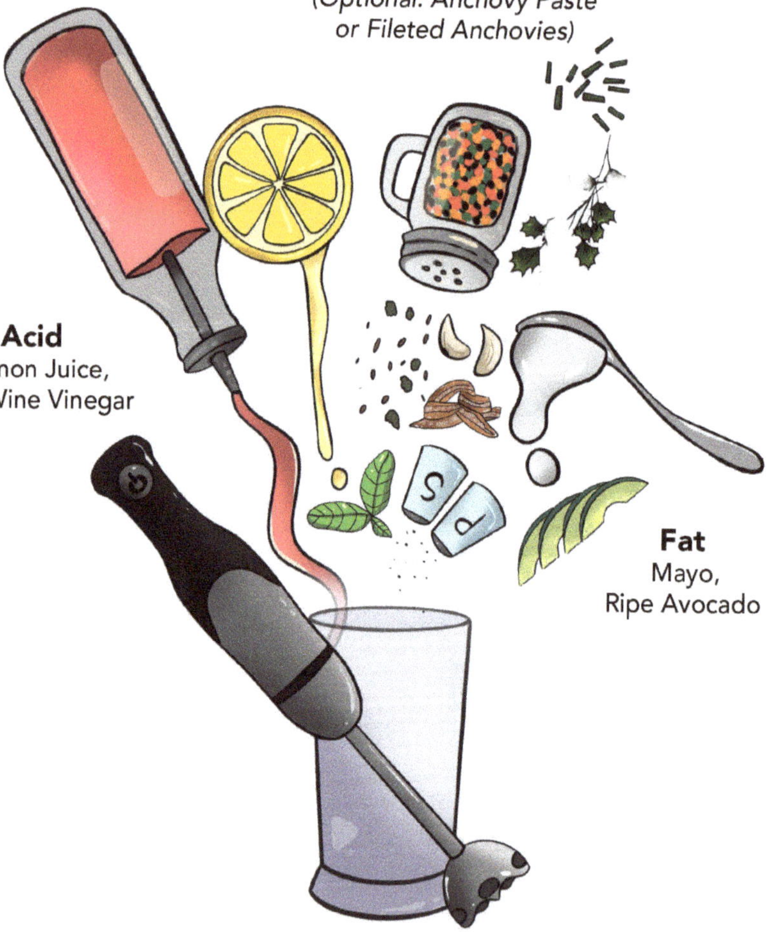

Acid
Lemon Juice,
Red Wine Vinegar

Fat
Mayo,
Ripe Avocado

Use Immersion Blender
(or Food Processor)

Peanut-Lime Dressing

Note: Typically lasts in the fridge for 4-5 days
when stored in airtight container.

Yum
Brown Sugar *(or Honey/Maple Syrup)*,
Garlic,
Fresh Ginger,
Soy Sauce,
Water *(to thin as needed)*,
(Optional: Sriracha or Chili Flakes for heat)

Acid
Lime Juice

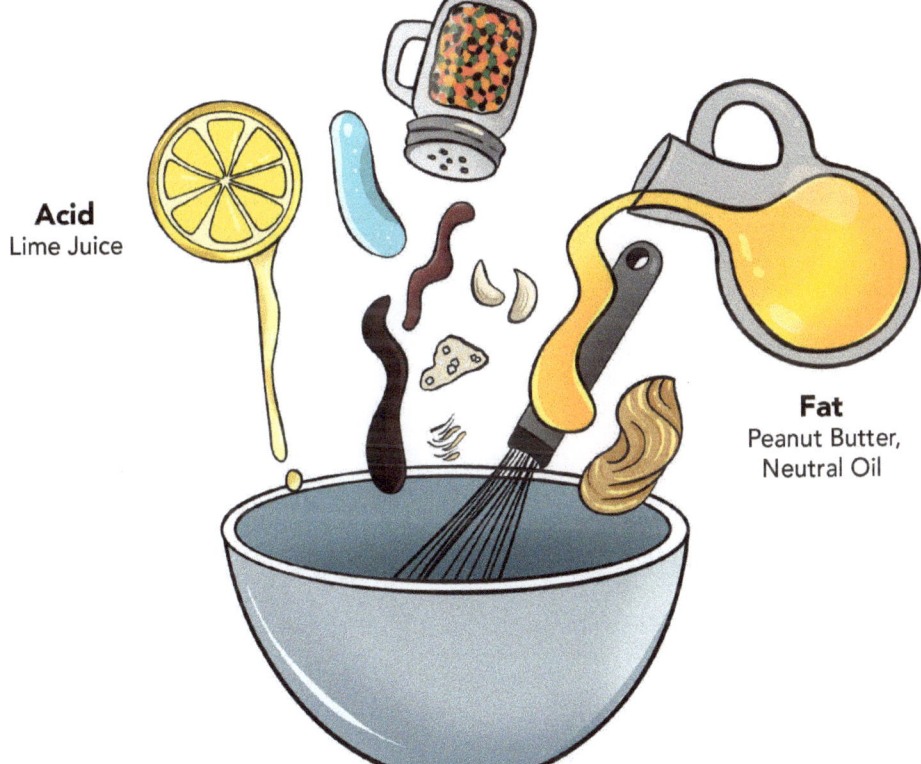

Fat
Peanut Butter,
Neutral Oil

Whisk in Bowl
(or use Immersion Blender for Extra Creamy Texture)

Create Your Signature Sauce

No Rules, Just Flavor

You've learned the formula — now it's your time to freestyle.
Let your fancy taste buds call the shots — jot down your custom combo below!

Name Your Creation _____

Chapter 5

Flavor Tweaks & Freestyle Magic

Let's talk about what separates a good dressing from a *"whoa, what IS this"*?! kind of dressing: tasting, adjusting, and being bold enough to freestyle.

This is where you stop second-guessing yourself and start creating from instinct.

The Golden Rule of Dressing Magic - *Taste as you go. Adjust. Repeat.*

That's it — seriously. The real secret to mastering dressings isn't memorizing a bunch of recipes.

It's knowing how to taste, how to trust your own preferences, and how to adjust until it hits just right. That's the mark of a confident home cook — and it's totally within your reach.

Your first mix might be too tangy, too flat, or missing "something." Don't toss it — tweak it.

Here's your cheat sheet to fix common flavor issues like a pro — no panic, no waste, just a few small tweaks that can save (or elevate!) your dressing in seconds:

Flavor Tweak Cheat Sheet

If your dressing is…

Too Sour: Add a touch of sweetener (honey, maple, agave) or mellow it out with a bit more oil or something creamy (mayo, yogurt, avocado). You're not fixing — you're balancing like a boss.

Too Oily: Add more acid (vinegar or lemon juice) or even a splash of water to cut the grease. A spoonful of mustard works like a charm, too — it's the kitchen's peacemaker.

Too Salty: Don't panic! Sweeten it up, splash in some acid, or mellow it with oil. Dairy like yogurt or sour cream can come to the rescue — they're the smooth talkers of the flavor world.

Too Bitter: A little honey or maple can work wonders. Or dilute with water and add more oil. Dijon mustard is your undercover superhero — it adds tang and flair that can smooth out bitterness.

Too Blah: Time to wake it up! Add a dash of mustard, fresh herbs, minced garlic, a sprinkle of chili flakes — and definitely salt or acid. Salt is like the fairy dust of flavor. Just a pinch and boom — magic.

Too Spicy: Don't sweat it (literally). Add something creamy or sweet to calm the heat. Yogurt or sour cream are like the spa treatment your tongue needs. A little acid can also slice through the spice.

Too Sweet: Bring in the acid! A splash of vinegar or citrus will balance things out. Salt and mustard also add depth and zing that can tone things down while still keeping the flavor fun.

Bottom line? Taste, tweak, and trust your tongue. You're the boss of your bowl.

Remix Inspiration Station

Once you've nailed the basics, it's time to remix like a pro. Don't just stick to the usual — explore flavor combos that surprise and delight. You can stir in sweet, spicy, tangy, nutty, or creamy extras to create something uniquely yours.

Here are some fun directions to spark your next masterpiece:

Garlic & Herb Goddess

⟶ Add fresh or roasted garlic, parsley, dill, chives
⟶ Great with Greek yogurt or buttermilk

Citrus Sunshine

⟶ Orange, lemon, lime, even grapefruit juice
⟶ Add zest for more punch!

Zesty Southwest

⟶ Lime juice, chipotle powder, cilantro
⟶ Pairs well with avocado or olive oil base

Green & Creamy Dreamy

⟶ Add avocado, cucumber, mint, and lemon
⟶ Blend until silky!

Sweet & Spicy Asian-Inspired

⟶ Rice vinegar, sesame oil, soy sauce, honey, ginger
⟶ Add sriracha for a little kick

Savory Cheese Bomb

⟶ Crumble in feta, blue cheese, or parmesan
⟶ Great in creamy or vinaigrette-style bases

Nutty & Nice

⇒ Stir in tahini or peanut butter

⇒ Adds rich, nutty depth to creamy or citrusy dressings

Fruit-Forward Fun

⇒ Mash berries or add roasted fruit

⇒ Sweetens things up with a juicy, tangy twist

Final Tip: There's No "Wrong," Just "Not Yet Right"

Every dressing is a little journey — and guess what? You don't need permission to change course mid-shake.

If you taste it and it's not quite there, don't sweat it — just tweak it! You're not messing up — you're experimenting, leveling up, and building serious flavor confidence.

Every spoonful brings you closer to mastering your kitchen — one fearless drizzle at a time. Keep stirring, keep tasting, and trust that you've got this.

Pro Move: Write It Down!

Keep a notebook or use the printable Flavor Journal in the back of this book. When you stumble onto something amazing, trust me — you'll want it saved for a repeat performance.

Give your dressing a name. Make it yours. *You're not just cooking — you're creating.*

Let's Recap:

Trust your taste buds. They are your #1 kitchen tool.

Don't be afraid to adjust — even a drop can make a difference.

Play with profiles, swap out ingredients, and make it yours.

This chapter isn't about being perfect — it's about being you.

Chapter 6

Confidence in a Jar

You did it — you rocked the kitchen! You whipped up vinaigrettes and creamy creations like a total pro. Now let's talk about keeping them fresh, pairing them brilliantly, and using them way beyond leafy greens. Because, let's be honest, your flavor game deserves to shine on *everything*.

Storing Your Dressings Like a Boss

Homemade dressings don't last forever (because yay, no weird preservatives!), but with the right storage, you'll get the most out of every delicious drop. No matter the type, store your dressings in an airtight container in the fridge to keep those flavors fresh and fabulous!

Vinaigrettes: These usually last up to 2 weeks. But if you've added fresh garlic, herbs, or citrus juice, plan to enjoy them within a few days. Just think: the more delicate the ingredient, the shorter the shelf life. And don't worry if it separates — vinaigrettes love a good shake. No drama, just swirl and serve.

Creamy Dressings with Dairy (yogurt, sour cream, etc.): Best used within 3–5 days. If it thickens in the fridge (especially Caesar-style), add a splash of water or milk and give it a good stir.

Mayo-Based Dressings: If you're using *homemade* mayo with fresh eggs, use within 1 week. If you've used *store-bought* mayo, you've got a bit more wiggle room — up to 2 weeks.

Pro Tip: Label your jars with the date and the name of your dressing. Even culinary goddesses (and rockstars) need a little reminder of what they whipped up and when!

Dressing It Up: What to Pair with What

Let's matchmake! Here's a quick cheat sheet for pairing dressings with different ingredients and meals:

Citrus or Champagne Vinaigrettes: Leafy greens, grilled shrimp, quinoa bowls, roasted beets

Balsamic or Berry-Based Vinaigrettes: Arugula, goat cheese, strawberries, chicken, pecans

Garlicky Herb or Italian Vinaigrettes: Romaine, tomatoes, mozzarella, pasta salads, crusty bread

Avocado or Creamy Lime Dressings: Taco bowls, grilled corn, black beans, roasted sweet potatoes

Ranch, Blue Cheese, or Thousand Island: Crisp iceberg, buffalo wings, roasted cauliflower, burgers, veggie sticks

Honey Mustard or Maple Dijon: Chicken tenders (homemade or drive-thru — no judgment), roasted carrots, pretzels, grain bowls

Beyond the Salad Bowl

Homemade dressings are basically flavor-packed sauces — so don't be afraid to use them like one!

Drizzle. Dip. Dunk. Pour.

Drizzle over roasted veggies

Use as a dip for raw veggies, fries, or chicken

Pour over grain bowls or nourish bowls

Spread onto sandwiches or wraps

Spoon over fish or grilled meats

Stir into pasta salads or cold noodles

Seriously, once you start, you'll wonder why you ever limited them to just lettuce.

Final Note: Your Jar = Your Crown

Every time you make a dressing, you're practicing more than cooking.

You're learning how to adjust, how to trust yourself, and how to get creative in your own kitchen kingdom.

And that — my friend — is kitchen confidence in a jar.

Chapter 7

Kitchen Swagger Plan

Okay, kitchen rockstar — you've shaken, whisked, blended, and tasted your way through the wonderful world of dressings. Now what?

You *keep going*, that's what. And this time… with swagger.

This chapter is your game plan for keeping the momentum rolling — because confidence doesn't come from one great vinaigrette. It comes from **showing up, practicing**, and **trusting your taste buds** over and over again.

Here's Your Kitchen Swagger Plan:

Step 1: Make One Dressing Per Week
Pick one day each week (Salad Sundays, maybe?) to whip up a new dressing. Try a different acid. A new herb. A combo you've never thought of before.

Start small, build bold.

Step 2: Choose a Weekly Flavor Theme

Need inspiration? Try themes like:

Herb Week: Basil, cilantro, parsley, or dill

Global Flavors: Asian-inspired, Mediterranean, Mexican

Fruit Forward: Citrus, berries, or roasted fruit blends

Creamy Dreams: Buttermilk, yogurt, avocado vibes

Zesty Heat: Mustard, horseradish, or chili-infused creations

Stick to a theme and play within it. You'll build creative muscle *and* variety.

Step 3: Use Your Flavor Journal

Write it all down in the back of this book or start your own journal:

What did you make?

What did you love (or not)?

What would you change next time?

This isn't about rules — it's about noticing what *you* like and how *you* like to cook.

Step 4: Pair It Differently Each Time

Sure, your vinaigrette rocked on that spinach salad... but what happens when you drizzle it over roasted sweet potatoes? Or a wrap? Or spooned onto a grain bowl?

Every dressing has a double life — go find it.

Step 5: Celebrate Every Win (and "Meh")

Not every creation will be magic — but every jar you shake is progress.

You showed up. You stirred something. That's what real flavor artists do — they don't aim for perfection every time, they aim to grow, experiment, and trust their taste.

Bottom line?

You don't need to master every dressing on the planet. Just keep tweaking. Keep tasting. Keep playing.

And keep chasing *your* perfect flavor profile — the one that makes your taste buds dance.

Because every time you stir things up your way, you're not just making a dressing — you're ditching the recipe training wheels and building kitchen swagger for life.

You Did It!

Look at you, kitchen rockstar! You didn't just flip through a few pages and call it a day — you showed up, whisked like a boss, trusted your taste buds, and leveled up your kitchen game one jar at a time.

You've learned the magic of homemade dressings, the art of emulsions, and how to build flavor without fear (or measuring spoons).

More importantly?

You've proven that creating delicious salad dressings is creative, empowering, and seriously fun — even if you splash a little too much vinegar or get a bit heavy-handed with the garlic now and then.

But hey — if you're thinking, "This was fun... what's next?"

I've got you covered.

Want to become a full-on Salad-Making Rockstar?

Check out my signature program, *Rock the Kitchen 101* — where we go way beyond the jar. You'll learn:

Game-changing techniques and core cooking methods (that don't rely on recipes!)

Salad types and the 5 keys to building a perfect, flavor-packed bowl

Knife handling and cuts, flavor profiles, the mighty taste palette, plating, garnishing — and oh yeah, some impressive but crazy-easy salad companions like soup, pasta, and fresh bread.

In other words? It's where confidence meets creativity — and your inner chef gets unleashed.

Special Reader Gift:

Use code **DRESSITUP** at checkout to get **20% off** the regular price!

Check it out at **www.rockthekitchen.net** and let's keep the flavor adventure rolling.

And hey, let's do each other a little flavor-fueled favor:

If you had fun rocking the kitchen with me, and feel it's well deserved, a quick review on Amazon or wherever you snagged your copy would be the cherry on top!

Your review helps others discover this book — and it seriously means the world to me.

As a thank-you, I've got a special bonus for you:

Get instant access to my "Salad Swagger: 5 Bold Bowls to Rock Your Plate" — 5 easy, delicious salads you can whip up fast to keep your momentum going strong!

Visit www.rockthekitchen.net/saladbonus to grab your special gift— or scan the QR code below

Scan Me
TO GRAB YOUR SALAD BONUS

Thanks for being part of this flavor-loving, spoon-wielding adventure.

Bonus

My Flavor Journal

Use these pages to jot down your genius! Every time you whip up a dressing, make it an experience — taste, tweak, and take notes. This is where flavor freedom truly begins.

Date: _____

Name of My Dressing: _____

What I Used:

    Oil: _____

    Acid: _____

    Yums (Flavor Boosters):

    _____

    _____

    _____

    _____

What I Loved:

    _____

    _____

    _____

    _____

What I'd Change Next Time:

_____

_____

_____

_____

What I Paired It With:

_____

_____

_____

_____

Next Time I Might Try:

_____

_____

_____

_____

Final Note

"No one is born a great cook — one learns by doing."

— Julia Child

About the Author

Kerstin Decook is a leadership coach, award-winning author, speaker, and unapologetic culinary enthusiast. She's the founder and flavor mentor behind Rock the Kitchen, where she helps home cooks ditch recipe fear, embrace flavor freedom, and actually have fun in the kitchen — one bold bite at a time.

But cooking wasn't always her thing.

Her path has been anything but ordinary — from a childhood behind the Iron Curtain in Russian-occupied East Germany to charting a life of adventure as a social educator, real estate agent, team manager, property wrangler, leadership coach, and eventually First Mate and Chef de Cuisine aboard the charter yacht she and her husband ran in the dreamy San Juan Islands.

It was during those yacht adventures that Kerstin realized... spaghetti and meatballs weren't gonna cut it. So she trained in culinary arts across the U.S., Canada, and Europe, diving deep into the *why* of good food — not just the how.

Now, she's on a mission to help thousands of home cooks feel proud, creative, and completely in control of what they serve.

Through her workshops, books, and a kitchen bubbling with love, laughter, and a whole lotta flavor, Kerstin helps women — and the bold men who dare — cook up a life that's as delicious as it is fulfilling.

Check out more at RockTheKitchen.net and BreakLooseAndFly.com

www.ingramcontent.com/pod-product-compliance
Lightning Source LLC
Chambersburg PA
CBHW041540120626
46551CB00019B/2780